Spirit Guides

Communicating with Your Unseen Friends

by

Victoria Young

Silver Forest Publishing
Boulder, Colorado

Cover Design by Rome
Cover Art by Lycia Harrison Adams

1st Printing
December 1988

Silver Forest Publishing
P. O. Box 3197
Boulder, CO 80307

This book, tape and box were printed and manufactured in the United States of America.

Dedication

This book is dedicated to the Divine Universal
Energy that resides in all of us.

Spirit Guides

Acknowledgements

I am very pleased to be able to thank and acknowledge those who contributed to this work. I feel blessed to have been able to work with such a talented group of people. They made it special for me.

My good friend, Julie Dickson gave of herself by proof-reading the book and making major contributions to the cover and the interior design of the book. She also deserves thanks for her expert advise on what works regarding packaging for book stores. We have also logged untold hours discussing metaphysical concepts.

Lycia Adams painted the original painting used on the cover. She worked hard to give me exactly what I wanted for the book.

Doctor Lou wrote and performed the original music on both sides of the tape. He, too, worked hard to give me the exact sound I wanted.

Lior Zelmanowicz owns Sound Set Studios, where we recorded the tape. Lior worked painstakingly to produce exactly the tape I wanted, even though what I was trying to accomplish was foreign to him . (Most recording studios are accustomed to recording 4 to 5 minute songs. They also record the music first. We did 22 minute songs and had to record the words first so that the music could be made to fit them.) It took a great deal of patience on his part.

My soul-brother, John Mark Bray deserves thanks for having helped me many years ago to discover what it felt like for me when I was working with my guides. And he deserves thanks for being such a wonderful, loving "little brother".

The Bishops of the Church of Tzaddi, Amy Kees and Dorothe Blackmere provided me with an atmosphere to meet other people with the same interests. I took a couple of their classes and they provided me with a launching pad to assimilate ideas and feelings. They have done this for many people and deserve much gratitude.

I also want to thank Hans Christian King, a medium who has acted as sort of a "mentor" for me. He always has unconditional love and encouraging words for me (as well as his other clients). During the times when I would get frustrated, he kept a little flame of light shining within.

And last, but not least, my dear friend and business partner, Richard Mitz. Richard has shown faith in me like no one before him. He has been extremely supportive of me and the project, and has contributed many ideas and concepts. Richard has taught me many priceless lessons regarding friendship. I cannot imagine it possible to have a better friend. In addition, it is his golden voice you hear on both sides of the tape.

Spirit Guides

Preface

I have been doing readings and teaching metaphysical classes for years. Something I have noticed consistently from my clients and students throughout the years is the nearly complete lack of confidence in their own ability to contact guides.

Almost without exception, they have a pre-conceived notion of what it is like to be psychic or what it is like to channel or what it is like to contact a guide. What ever that notion is, they perceive it as something outside themselves or impossible for them to do. They think that whatever it takes to do all this is something they haven't got.

As a result, I developed a class several years ago aimed specifically at that issue. The class was called "Working with Spirit Guides." The class was aimed at teaching people how to recognize their own way of contacting a guide. Much time was given to dispelling the beliefs about there only being certain ways to experience contact with guides.

At the beginning of each class, I would ask each student to tell the class why he/she was there and what he/she wanted to learn. A majority of students in each class would say they didn't think they really had the "talent" it took to contact a guide. They would say they weren't psychic enough or they couldn't relax and meditate or they couldn't visualize a guide, etc.

What I discovered was that each of these people had plenty of ability to do exactly what I was doing. Their methods or their style or how they experienced it might have been profoundly different from mine, but they were contacting their guides, all the same. That was the real power of the class. The students left the class knowing that they, too, have the ability to contact and work with their guides.

This book and its accompanying tape are the natural outgrowth of teaching that class for several years. Everyone of the students who thought he or she could not contact guides was a teacher to me. Each one of them showed me another aspect of the many different paths available to be taken to the same goal.

It is my sincere desire that you feel empowered by reading this book. For what I hope to do is show you that the power to contact guides is within you.

Spirit Guides

Table of Contents

How to Use

the Book and Tape

Spirit Guides

Chapter One

How to Use the Book and Tape

You may find it easier and more enjoyable to begin contacting your guides if you use the book and tape in a certain manner. We created this as a book and tape because we think it is important for you to have the instruction and theory of the book combined with the experience provided by the tape. There are currently several fine books on the market regarding work with spirit guides and channeling. Having only a book poses some difficulty, however. The difficulty for the reader is that he/she has to try to remember each of the steps to go through (left brain activity) while trying to immerse the self in the experience (right brain activity).

If you are in the middle of a visualization

and you have to stop the visualization to remember what you are supposed to do or see next, you may have trouble getting back into the visualization. However, if you have someone guiding you on tape, you can relax, let go, and let the voices on the tape take care of the left brain activity while you allow yourself to get involved in the experience.

A tape alone doesn't handle everything, however. There are many good tapes with guided meditations out on the market. The potential problem here is that working with spirit guides is a relatively new realm for many people. They don't know what they should be experiencing. They don't know what is "normal". They need to have many more issues addressed than just going through a guided meditation. If this were a guided meditation on getting rid of headaches, it would be simpler. You already know what it should be like to "cure" a headache. You know how it feels to have a headache and how it feels not to have a headache. Therefore, the guided meditation wouldn't need a lot of additional literature. A guided meditation to experience something you have never experienced before is quite different. It needs plenty of support literature so you can feel comfortable going through the meditations.

Before using the tape, we strongly suggest that you read a good portion of the book. Chapters of special importance include:

Why Contact Spirit Guides?

What is a Spirit Guide?

Does Everyone Have Spirit Guides?

What Forms do Guides Take?

Why is a Guide with You?

How does it Feel to Work with a Guide?

Preparation to Work with Your Guides.

About the Meditations.

If you have special concerns or fears about working with guides, you should read the chapter entitled *Overcoming Fears and Resistance* thoroughly.

If you have used the tape and are having problems in certain areas, then you should read the chapter called *Trouble Shooting Problems.*

If you feel you are ready to meet a new guide or that a change in guidance is taking place for you, then you should read the chapter on *New Guides*.

When you are ready to begin using the second side of the tape regularly, I suggest you read the chapter called *Channeling.*

I strongly recommend that you read the first group of seven chapters listed above before you begin with the tape. It should only take you an hour or two to read them and they will give you a lot of much needed preparation. We can always use any extra help we can get when dealing with areas new and unfamiliar to us.

Eventually, you may want to read all the chapters in the book, but of course, it is not necessary. Some of them may pertain to you and some may not. Some of them, such as the chapters on channeling may be interesting to you as a matter of curiosity. And then again, you may wish to use them to develop your own channeling abilities.

Why Contact

Spirit Guides?

8

Chapter Two

Why Contact Spirit Guides?

When I completed my first draft of this book, I showed it to Lycia Adams, the artist who did the painting on the cover of this book. I wanted to explain to her exactly what the book was about so that she would have a better idea of what the cover needed to represent. After I went through a twenty minute explanation of what was in the book and how I approached each item, she asked an innocent question. "Is there anywhere in the book where you talk about why people work with guides and how they benefit?"

She wasn't trying to be critical. She just noticed an obvious omission. I have been working with guides for so long that I tend to take it for granted that everyone knows why we do it and what benefits we reap. I'm glad I had her fresh point of view. With that in mind, I offer the following as my ideas on why we work with guides and what benefits we derive from such work.

Greater Peace of Mind and ability to cope with our day-to-day lives.   I have found that my work with guides has definitely helped me to be much more peaceful and calm. People who knew me from a long time ago talk about a new peacefulness and contentedness they see in me now. I assure you, this was not the case in my past. I also receive many reports from others who work with guides and they have the very same results. They are more relaxed and happier with their lives. Their life circumstances may or may not have changed, but they have become much more centered in their dealings with everyday life.

This is partly because there is a certain peace that automatically comes from meditation in almost any form. When you allow yourself the opportunity to meditate and alter your consciousness, you drop the worries about your daily life, even if it is only for a few moments at a time. The dropping of all that worry-baggage creates a space for you to experience peace, even if it is only brief. If you begin to do this daily, it has a gradual, but profound effect on you, for those little gaps compound a bit and you begin to experience greater peace.

As you contact guides, you also begin to find a sense of peace, well-being and security which comes from knowing you have access to more wisdom and information than you previously thought. Knowing you have more resources creates a greater sense of peace.

Greater Perception of what is really going on in your life. After a while, you will begin to look at the circumstances in your life from a more aware point of view. Working with your guides helps you to develop and increase your awareness. You will find that you are aware in more depth of what is going on in the situations around you. You will find that you are more able to look beyond the "symptoms" or the "story" of a situation to what is really going on. This greater perception allows you to reinforce your sense of peace and well being.

Better Ability to Handle Stressful Situations that arise in your life. As you develop greater peace of mind and greater perception of what is going on, you also begin to be a little "detached" from your situations. This detachment or ability to stand back a little from what is happening enables you to handle your problems more easily. You become less overwhelmed by your problems because you are less attached to certain aspects of them that you used to be. Many people I have met in the business world have told me they use some sort of meditation or work with their guides in order to bring them enough peace to get through an extremely stressful work day. (Though most of them would not admit it publicly, as it is still frowned upon in the mainstream business world. I wonder if corporations will some day recognize that some of their top performers are top performers because of their ability to detach themselves through meditation and work with guides.)

Development of Talents you have been working on. My artist friend has really developed her art far more fully by using her metaphysical skills and drawing energy from her guides and the guides of people for whom she paints. I have another book in the works which was written by me in close collaboration with one of my guides. I know of many other people who use the inspiration from their guides to develop existing or even previously untried talents.

What is a

Spirit Guide?

Spirit Guides

Chapter Three

What is a Spirit Guide?

Almost everyone you ask will give you a different definition of what they think a spirit guide is. Because most people have very specific and precise definitions of what constitutes a spirit guide, they create a barrier between themselves and their guides. By being precise, they are limiting a spirit guide to being only what is within that precise definition. Any time you create a limited notion of what something is or how something works, then you automatically limit your ability to experience it. If, for instance, you decide all spirit guides must look or act a certain way and in your meditation you encounter entities that don't fit your definition, then you will decide you did not experience a spirit guide. You will say that was your imagination instead.

Some people believe spirit guides are disincarnate souls. That is, souls which are not currently in a body. This is probably the most common belief (and therefore the most common experience) of people working with spirit guides. When you have this belief, you experience your guides as being entities separate from yourself.

Still other people believe spirit guides are really your higher self and that you are tapping into higher wisdom within yourself. This belief will create an experience in which you are the source of the information you receive from your guides. In this instance you will not experience your guides as separate from yourself. Instead, you will experience them as a higher, wiser part of yourself.

Another less common belief is that we all have parallel lives. This means your soul is much vaster and occupies many other bodies besides just the one in which you experience yourself at this time. Some people believe these parallel lives are all occurring in the very same time and space as you are currently experiencing. Others believe these parallel lives are not limited to just this time and space and that you have portions of your soul in other times and places as well. Many with this belief draw the conclusion that you don't really have "past" and "future" lives , but all of your lives are occurring simultaneously all of the time. This belief is how they explain the possibility of "time travel" and also how one easily "tunes in" to these other lives. People with this belief find that when they are experiencing communication with spirit guides, those guides are really parallel lives of their own. In some ways, it can seem like a twist on the notion that you are working with your higher self. Both ideas identify the source of the information and wisdom received as an aspect of yourself.

It really does not matter whether you adopt one of the beliefs stated above or if you have an entirely separate belief. It is important, however, to understand that what you believe will shape what you experience. I suggest that you may wish to begin your work with your mind as open as possible. This will enable you to have a less limited scope in which to work. The less limited your scope, the more likely you are to begin to experience work with your guides.

Spirit Guides

Does Everyone

Have Spirit Guides?

Spirit Guides

Chapter Four

Does Everyone
Have Spirit Guides?

Once in a while I encounter a person who wishes to work with a spirit guide but is somehow convinced he/she doesn't have a guide. I find invariably that this is really because of a block the person has. He may doubt his ability to contact a guide or to receive information. Or she may feel she is not "important" enough to have a guide.

I believe everyone has guides. I have yet to see an exception to this. Even people with fairly strong blocks to accessing their guides can be helped to experience contact with their guides. Some blocks are stronger (and therefore may take longer) than others, but they all can be overcome. Of course, if a person resolutely believes he does not have any guides and therefore never accesses their energy, then he effectively doesn't have the guidance.

Anyone who wishes to work with spirit guides will find that she is able to do so with just a little training. If a person's blocks are particularly strong, she may have to practice the exercises given in the training a few extra times in order to feel successful. However, there is no extra rigorous training for her.

Even if you are having difficulty accessing your guides, please assume for now that you do indeed have guides. This will allow you to remain open enough to experience your guides more easily. Once you overcome your blocks and actually experience your guides, you will have your own personal memories and reference points to call upon and therefore make it easier and easier to access your guides.

What Forms

do Guides Take?

Spirit Guides

Chapter Five

What Forms do Guides Take?

People who work with their spirit guides report that they come in many different forms. In the classes I have taught, people have had a surprisingly wide variety of experiences. By far and away, most of them experience their guides as being like a "person". Within this general category of "person", they report many different types of identities.

Following is a listing of the most common types of "persons" which are experienced as guides:

Relatives - Usually a deceased parent or grandparent. (Sometimes it is a deceased brother, sister or ancestor other than parent or grandparent.) This form is quite common, especially because people feel love and a close bond with such deceased relatives. Most people also feel they can more easily trust a relative than a stranger.

Mythical Persons - These are "people" who are reputed to have lived in our myths and religions. These people may or may not have lived on this earth, but I call them "mythical" because there is no real proof. However, they seem to be very alive because of our cultural traditions. Examples of such people are Merlin the Magician, King Arthur, Jesus Christ, the Virgin Mary, Quan Yin, Buddha, members of the White Brotherhood etc. Some less specific examples of this category could be fairies, devas, and the "little people".

Famous Persons - These are people who are historical figures. They attained some fame during their lives on earth and are still, now highly thought of. Examples of such people are Albert Einstein, Nicola Tesla, Mohandas K. Gandhi, Dr. Martin Luther King, John F. Kennedy, Joan of Arc, Queen Elizabeth I, Madame Curie, etc.

Unknown Persons - These are people

never encountered before in this life. They may take male, female or sexless identities. (Though I find that the vast majority of people who experience their guides as "persons" feel more comfortable if they perceive their guide as either male or female.) These guides may have names as simple and common as Fred or Linda, or as exotic as Tovar, Atrilonia, Sung tu. (Some of the well known guides who are channeled might fit into this category. They have names such as Ramtha, Mafu, Seth, Michael, Lazaris.)

Native Americans - I have had many students who experience their guides as American Indians. They come from various tribes and seem to be equally distributed between male and female. They have names such as Tall White Tree, Singing Water, Little Bear, etc.

Space Brothers - Some people report experiencing guides who are from other planets. Sometimes they feel these guides are physically incarnate. Others may feel the guides exist in another dimension and are therefore not physical as we know it. A fairly well-known guide who is channeled by a man in Los Angeles is called Bashar. I feel that Bashar falls into this category.

There are a couple of other categories in

which people commonly experience their guides. However, these do not conveniently fit under the general category of "persons". Following is a listing of those categories:

Totem Animals - These are animals which have traditionally been given mystical powers under certain traditions. The most common traditions to recognize totem animals are Native American ones or other shamanistic traditions. Certain animals, such as the bear, mountain lion, eagle, hawk, etc., have been adopted as "totems" by various tribes and individuals. The clan referred to in the title of the book *Clan of the Cave Bear* was a group who had taken the cave bear as their totem animal. Occasionally a person who is trying to contact a spirit guide experiences that guide as a totem animal.

Mythical Animals - these are animals which don't physically exist in this world as we know it. (Or at least there is no physical evidence of them.) Common examples of these animals are unicorns, Pegasus, dragons, etc. Some people find that experiencing these magical, mystical animals with unusual powers is very exciting.

Other Animals - These are mostly animals one would find on the earth today. I know a woman who has a cute little gray and white rabbit for a guide. A man I know has a fawn (baby deer), and yet another has a male African lion. These are not all that uncommon, but it sometimes takes the person quite a while to recognize that this animal which keeps appearing in his meditations is a guide.

Inanimate Guides - These are a little harder for people to sometimes recognize. In one class I taught, a man encountered a leaf which clung to his elbow. He said it gave him a very comforting feeling. Another person I know finds guidance and inspiration from a tree which she calls "Grandfather Tree". These are guides which do not have the animation of all the others listed above. However, lack of animation does not mean lack of effectiveness as a guide.

Light Forms - These are lights which may appear as balls, human shape, large ovals, or any other shape. They can be in any color you can imagine. A person may encounter a light form which gives him/her great wisdom and comfort. Sometimes the light form seems to glow brighter, change shapes and colors or pulsate when giving information to the recipient.

Invisible Energy - Once in a while a person will sense the presence of a guide but have no form at all to connect it with. There is just a knowing that the guide is there. The lack of form does not make this type of guide any less real. In many ways, the person could actually be making clearer contact because he/she is not in need of all the various trappings to create a guide which seems real. The Taoist philosophy states that anything which becomes defined or explained loses some of its real meaning in the process of trying to confine it to a definition.

Why is a Guide

with You?

Spirit Guides

Chapter Six

Why is a Guide with You?

A question I frequently am asked in class is "How long has this guide been with me?" People want to know if their guides have been with them since birth or whether they showed up at a certain age or for a certain reason.

I have found as I worked with many people that the length of time the guide is with them and the reason the guide is there often correspond. Therefore, I have made my own categories related to this. They are as follows:

Lifetime Guide - This is the guide who has been with you since birth and will be there until you pass over to the other side. Everyone

Spirit Guides

I have encountered had at least one of these guides and many had more than one. This guide is akin in nature to what many people refer to as your Guardian Angel. The one who looks over you, helps, comforts and generally protects you is your Lifetime Guide. Most people find this the most comforting guide of all because of the security that comes with the feeling that this guide is always there. No matter what else comes and goes in their lives, these people feel they at least have this one constant they can count on.

Lesson Guide - This is a guide who is here to help you work on a particular lesson. This lesson may be to be less harsh in judging others, or to learn your own independence, or to learn about unconditional love, etc. This guide will often have certain qualities which help to learn that lesson. For instance, if your guide is here to teach you about compassion for others, then the guide may be very gentle and compassionate itself. The length of duration for a lesson guide can be as long or as short as necessary. However, they don't generally leave at the first sign of progress. We humans have such strong habit of making progress, then sliding backwards a little, then making some more progress, then sliding again, that a guide doesn't disappear the first time it appears we have mastered a lesson. That guide is here for as long as it takes to truly make that lesson a part of us.

Project Guide - This is a guide who is here to help you with a specific project. That project can be to get your college degree, or to write a book, or to begin a particular career, or to start a certain relationship. Not every project we undertake will necessarily be assisted by a guide. But there are certain ones which are important to our own growth and development. Those are the kind that are helped by the nurturing of a guide. Again, the duration of this guide's presence is variable, depending on how long it takes us to get on with the project. Usually, these guides are not around as long as a lesson guide (unless the person being helped is a procrastinator) because projects tend to have more definite beginning and ending points.

Emergency Guide - This is a guide that is here for an emergency situation. I used to call these guides 'Trauma Helpers", but the name didn't have as much meaning for students as "Emergency Guide". I believe these are the kind of guides who help people through dire situations, such as automobile accidents ("there's no way he should have survived that"), critical illnesses, and other emergencies. We all hear stories such as the one about a man who is driving down the road and suddenly hears a woman's voice calling for help on his car radio. Somehow he is able to follow the voice and finds the woman buried in an avalanche under ten feet of snow. She had no radio broadcasting device with her, but he "miraculously" heard her voice on his radio. I believe such incidents are a result of an intervening spirit guide of this category.

Drop-In Guide - This is probably the hardest type of guide to explain, because it isn't as predictable as the others. This guide is almost what you would call the "all-others" category. A drop in guide can be one which shows up to give you an inspirational message and then leaves right away. It can also be a guide which appears to be around sporadically. It can be a guide that you are aware of one time only. Or it can be a guide that you are aware of periodically.

How does it Feel

to Contact a Guide?

Spirit Guides

Chapter Seven

How Does it Feel to Contact a Guide?

Lots of people think that when we are truly contacting guides we will see and hear them very clearly with our physical eyes and ears. They expect to see an apparition and hear its distinct voice just as Luke Skywalker did with Obi-wan Kenobe. Then, when these people don't experience anything of the kind, they begin to think they can't do it or they just don't have the mystical gift that it takes to "see" and "hear".

I put those two words in quotes for a reason. Very few people I know are truly able to see spirits with their eyes or hear them with their ears. Even among professional mediums it is extremely rare. However, because of the limitations of our language, you will find people who experience working with their guides talk about it in terms of "hearing" and "seeing". They will say things such as "I had this vision and in it I saw...." Even during a reading you'll find a medium saying "What I'm hearing for you is...." In a sense, what they really do is "see" with their "mind's eye" and "hear" an "inner voice". The fact is, our language has no better words to accurately (and briefly) describe what is going on. Because of this many people think they should be able to hear and see with their ears and eyes when making contact with spirit guides.

If your own expectation is that you should be able to see them clearly with your eyes and hear them clearly with your ears, then you will probably find your experience disappointing. In fact, you will probably think that you did not experience anything — even though you did. When you first "see" with your mind's eye or "hear" an inner voice, you will most likely want to dismiss it as imagination.

Physical Clues

Working with guides is often very subtle. Only little nuances give it away at first. Sometimes your first clues are how you feel physically. When I was first receiving messages from my spirit guides, I would feel a little numbness in the middle of my forehead (my third eye). I would find myself sitting there and rubbing my forehead as if to bring back the feeling. It wasn't until someone else pointed out to me that I always did it that I realized what was going on. And there was a period of time when I was first channeling that I found myself always feeling just a bit light-headed when my guides had a message to give me. This was not the kind of light-headed where you feel you are going to pass out. It was the kind in which I entered an altered state of consciousness and therefore felt less connected and focused on the reality we perceive during our normal states of consciousness.

When I felt that way, I knew I was in a state in which I could more easily pull through information. I must caution readers, however, that you should never try to use drugs, alcohol or any other artificial means to achieve these states. All you will succeed in doing is causing damage to your body and havoc to your psychic centers. That will ultimately block your messages or garble them so that they are not clear.

Other symptoms reported by my students are:

1. Hearing a buzzing or clicking noise,

2. Feeling a tingling sensation,

3. Smelling a sweet perfume (which couldn't be explained normally),

4. Feeling as if someone is lightly tickling the top of the head or the ear or the nose,

5. Seeing a "light" or movement out of the corner of the eye,

6. Feeling the need to yawn a great deal (when not tired or sleepy).

You may find that you experience some of these physical sensations or none of them. You may experience some other sensations not mentioned here. Or you may experience none at all. It does not matter which sensations (if any) you experience. They are not indicators of how well you are doing. They only serve as signals to let you know you are making contact. And of course, it must be said that when a person experiences one of these sensations it does not necessarily mean that he is making contact with a guide. It all comes down to a matter of experience and your own intuitive sensing of what is going on.

If for example, every time you sit down to meditate and contact a guide you have a particular sensation or one of a few sensations that repeat themselves, then I would take it as a physical sign that you are making contact. However, absence of these signs does not mean that you are not making contact.

Imagination?

The most common response from people who begin to meditate and experience contact with their guides is that they think it is all just their imagination. In class once, a woman whose guide gave her the name "Stanley" said she thought it was just her imagination because it was a very common name she had heard many times. In that same class, a man who "heard" the name "Baruda" for his guide thought it was just his imagination because it was a name he had never heard before.

This doubt which manifests in the form of crediting the imagination is applied to literally every aspect of experiencing a guide. If, during meditation she "saw" an image of a person in a Grecian robe coming forward to talk to her, she will say her imagination made it up. If he finds himself transported during meditation to a place altogether different from the place where he was intending to go, he will say his imagination played a trick on him.

I remember many years ago when I was in a meditation class and the woman directing the class guided us all to go to a meadow and enjoy playing there. I had done this exercise before so I was familiar with what it was like for me to go to the meadow. However, instead of ending up in the meadow, I ended up flying through space and I arrived at a huge, beautiful palace made of what looked like quartz crystal. Everything about the place was enormous. The doors were easily 30 feet wide and 70 feet high. I walked into the palace and saw people walking around silently in monk's robes. As I would walk down corridors, the right doors would automatically open for me to enter. Everything was peaceful and somewhat awesome there. When I told the class leader about it later, she became upset. She said I had gone to a "very special place" and I wasn't allowed to go there anymore unless I went there under her guidance.

Of course, I wasn't intimidated by her admonishment. I figured that if I wasn't supposed to go there, I wouldn't have been able to get there in the first place. I visited the place a few more times after that. On several visits, I was given some information which I found very valuable. Obviously, my original visit there wasn't in form with where I thought I was going. However, I don't think it was just my imagination (I suppose it helped that the teacher seemed to know something about this place.) playing tricks on me.

Several years later, I was involved in a group meditation with about thirty people. When we finished our half hour silent, non-guided meditation, participants were asked if they would like to share what they experienced in meditation. One man said he felt very confused because he had ended up in this big crystal palace where the people walked around silently wearing monks robes! He had very little experience with metaphysics and had only begun to meditate a short time before. (He was the president of a computer firm and was more accustomed to a different sort of "reality".) He was sure that he had just experienced a trick of his imagination. Before I could speak to tell him I had been there before, another woman told him she knew the place well and that she considered it to be very special.

I find it very interesting that many of us

have found this place by "accident", having never heard of it before our first visit. The fact that so many of us find it is usually convincing proof that it is not imaginary. However, if you find yourself experiencing something that no one else seems to have experienced, it is no less real. (It is likely that you will eventually meet someone with the same or a very similar experience.)

Once again, I request that you try to keep as open a mind as possible at first. You will wish to ask the question numerous times, "Is this real or is it my imagination?" At first, try to keep the notion that it is just as likely to be real as your imagination.

Two Selves?

Many times, people report that listening to their spirit guides is like having "two selves" talking to each other (usually in thought form). It's as if you have two sides of your mind. One may be listening while the other is "talking", or they may be carrying on a "conversation", or even a "debate".

A long time ago, when I was a manager of seven departments in a major corporation, I had closeted myself to do budgets. I hated that part of the process so I locked myself in my office so I could do it without interruption and get it over with. As I was sitting there running endless adding machine tape, the thought came through my mind "Edgar Allan Poe". I shook it off and continued working. The thought kept coming back into my mind with great persistence. It continued for hours.

Eventually, I stopped my work and asked myself why I kept thinking about Edgar Allan Poe. Another thought came into my mind. It was, "You need to read some Edgar Allan Poe."

I thought in response, "I don't want to read Edgar Allan Poe, I don't even like him."

Again I thought, "Edgar Allan Poe was the master of the short story. You've been wanting to write some short stories. Reading Poe could help."

The thoughts went on, "I don't want to learn to write horror stories."

"You don't have to," I thought, "you can just notice the elements of a good short story and use them on whatever you want to write."

The back and forth "conversation with

myself" seemed like just that. Finally, I told myself I would read some Poe soon and I got back to work. At the end of the work day, I left my office to say goodnight to my employees. One of the men said he was going to a psychic fair and wanted to know if anyone else wanted to go. Of course, I volunteered. At the fair, I got a reading from an elderly woman. She suddenly looked at me with a start and asked me what I did for a hobby.

"I'm a writer." I replied.

"Do you like Edgar Allan Poe?" She asked innocently. Chills ran up and down my body.

"This is really strange. I haven't thought about Poe since we had to read him years ago in school and today I've been thinking about him all day." I said nervously.

"Well, dear, he's standing right behind you and he says he wants to help you write."

"I don't want to write the creepy stuff he wrote."

"You don't have to. He's willing to help you write anything you want. All you have to do is sit down with your tablet and ask Edgar Allan Poe to please help you."

Well, I left that event shaken but still very skeptical. A few days later when no one was in my house to witness my actions, I sat down with a tablet and said ,"Edgar Allan Poe, please help me." I quickly began to write a story about a man from another planet visiting earth. It wasn't macabre at all. The next day, a friend who also writes dropped by. I asked her to read my little story.

When she was finished, she said, "You know, it isn't the same language or the same style, but something about this story reminds me of Edgar Allan Poe." Again I got the chills.

I now believe that when I was sitting in my office that day having a "conversation" with myself about reading Poe, I was really communicating with a guide. I'm not sure if that guide was Poe, and I don't really care. What I am sure of is that what seemed like my mind playing "devil's advocate" was really communication with a guide.

I tell this story so that you will begin to notice during your work with guides, how it manifests in your mind. This feeling of two

---

parts of self "talking" in your mind is quite common. With practice you will begin to tell the difference between your own thoughts and communications from guides.

My guides use a more formal grammar and syntax than I do. They do not use contractions or slang. As a result, their messages seem a little more formal and stilted. This enables me to fairly easily tell the difference now.

Flashes

Sometimes the information from guides will come through in what I call a "flash". It is just a sudden knowing that you acquire. You may not see an image, hear a voice or even have a thought with this "flash". One moment you are not aware of something and the next moment you are. Many people report getting these "flashes" when they suddenly realize someone they know is pregnant, or in danger, or nearby.

All of you have undoubtedly had at least one of these experiences. Maybe you've had the sudden feeling that someone needs you. You call that person on the phone and find he was just getting ready to call you for help. Or you find yourself thinking about someone you haven't seen in years and a few hours later you run into her in the shopping mall. Or you suddenly have the urge to call a friend for "no reason" and your friend tells you he just got a big promotion at work and wants you to help him celebrate.

These flashes can be fairly innocuous or extremely important. If you take notice, you can start to track these flashes. As you give more emphasis to them, you will find them occurring more often.

Spirit Guides

Preparation to

Contact Your Guides

Spirit Guides

Chapter Eight

Preparation to Contact Your Guides

Contacting Spirit Guides does not require any expensive or extensive preparations. If you encounter people who are encouraging you to spend a lot of money or even a great deal of energy to prepare yourself to work with Spirit Guides, I suggest you walk away and don't do anything they ask.

People may try to tell you that you need special candles, incense, ointments, crystals, etc., in order to contact your guides. Your personal tastes may dictate that you use some of these things because you feel more comfortable with them. For instance, you may like the smell of an incense or the light of candles and find that it relaxes you. If so, go for it. However, keep in mind that it is your own energy and essence that is merging with the spirit guides, not the essence of the tools you use.

Environment

I find it is most helpful if your environment is free from as many distractions as possible. I like to use techniques to prevent interruptions and techniques to make sure I am comfortable so that I won't find my attention wandering to any discomfort. Therefore I do the following as a regular part of my routine when preparing to receive information from my guides:

1. Take the phone off the hook

2. Place "Do Not Disturb" sign on the door

3. Adjust lighting so it is not too bright

4. Choose a very comfortable chair

5. Wear loose, comfortable clothing

6. Play soft background music (with no voices and no real "tune")

In addition, I try to consciously choose the *time* when I work with my spirit guides. Choosing the time is often a major factor in setting the environment. If you choose a time when your house mate is having a loud party in the other room, or when a construction crew is running a jackhammer outside your window, or when you have a migraine headache, you are probably going to have very limited success (at best) contacting your guides and receiving clear information.

Late in the evening when the rest of the world is winding down and people are going off to sleep is often the best time of all to do this. Believe it or not, every person (even you and me) is broadcasting vibrations and energy patterns at full tilt when wide awake. Those vibrations, like radio waves, are around you constantly, even if you aren't consciously tuned in to them. You can't tell which radio waves are passing though your living room until you adjust the tuner on your radio or television to pick them up. It is the same with the broadcasting of other people. Late in the evening, there is less of their energy to provide interference between you and your guides.

I know some people who actually get up in the middle of the night — say around 3:00 AM

— to meditate and receive messages from their guides. They say this is the time of day when the rest of the world around them offers the least interference. I'm not suggesting that you need to do anything this extreme to achieve success. However, if you find yourself waking up around that time for no apparent reason, you might want to give it a try, especially if you are having any difficulty falling back to sleep. Usually, once you've meditated, you fall back to sleep very easily.

Physical

By physical, I mean the things you can do relative to your physical body to prepare for contacting your guide. Some of the following may be helpful for you:

1. Don't eat a heavy meal before meditating

2. Don't meditate feeling hungry

3. Stretch a little to get the "kinks" out

4. Breathe deeply

5. Relax as much as possible

6. Sit upright in a comfortable chair

7. Keep your feet flat on the floor

8. Avoid crossing your arms or legs

9. Wear loose, comfortable clothing

10. Remove eye glasses or contact lenses

11. Remove rings from fingers and any other "tight" jewelry

As you can see, the real emphasis is on being so comfortable that you won't be distracted by discomfort. However, the reason I suggest sitting up rather than lying down is so that you aren't so comfortable that you fall off to sleep. I suggest avoiding crossing any body parts so that your physical energy is running in a smooth "circuit" and not "bunched up" at the points where you cross your body. Some of this may seem like picking "nits". If it does to you, use your own discretion regarding the previous list. Remember, the goal is for you to be comfortable and relaxed. If anything on the list would interfere with your personal feeling of comfort, then forego that item.

Mental

Just as you need to be comfortable physically, it is very important to be comfortable mentally. Usually, this means clearing all the internal interference in the form of worries, doubts, fears, deep desires, etc. One of the main reasons I wanted to design this book as being an adjunct to a tape is that I find a tape with a guided meditation helps a great deal in clearing out unwanted mental noise. In order to follow the suggestions on the tape, you have to be mentally relaxed and paying attention to the directions given.

Listening to the tape and focusing on the voices helps to put all those other things aside for the time being. There are a few other things you can do, however. They include:

1. Grounding Meditation (detailed elsewhere in this book)

2. Allowing mind to go "out of focus"

3. Counting your breaths

4. Telling yourself that this is your uninterrupted time

5. Repeating your special affirmation

The last one on the list, repeating your special affirmation, is very helpful. I find that if you take some deep breaths and say in your mind, *"I openly and willingly receive my guide on the conscious plane,"* that it really helps. The reason I call it your "special" affirmation is that you can take the one I have given here and adjust it for your own comfort. When I am teaching a class, this is the one I have the students use during the exercise. I notice a great difference in the results when they use it. (When they don't use it, some of them have more difficulty making contact.)

At first, I suggest that you try some of the items listed above to adjust your environmental, physical and mental situations. Once you have tried them, you will probably wish to continue using them until you reach a point where you feel you don't need as much preparation.

Spirit Guides

About the

Meditations

Chapter Nine

About the Meditations

To begin the meditations, there are several things I suggest you do. First, you may wish to re-read the section on "Preparation". In addition, I suggest you do a grounding meditation at least the first few times you try to contact your guides. I would like to re-emphasize at this point the importance of using your special affirmation. If you don't have one, use the following: "I openly and willingly receive my guide on the conscious plane." Try saying this to yourself three or more times before you start.

Once you have made your preparations and have your tape turned on, this is what we will be suggesting:

Meeting Your Guide

The purpose of this meditation is to help you make contact with a guide and begin to feel what it is like to contact a guide. It can be used to meet your first guide for the very first time. It can also be used again and again to make your contact more clear. (Especially if you found your first attempt disappointing.) And of course, it is useful if you want to meet "new" guides from time to time.

First you will be doing some deep breathing. Then you will be asked to visualize a series of colored numbers (from 7 to 1) on the inside of your forehead. This is a countdown to help you relax. Once we have completed the countdown, you will be asked to visualize yourself in a beautiful meadow and to notice the kinds of plants and animals you see there as you enjoy yourself in that meadow. You will walk slightly downhill from the meadow into a beautiful enchanted forest. You will find the forest full of magical plants and animals. Everything around you is perfectly safe and enjoyable.

You will follow the path as it meanders through the forest. After a while you will come to a river. As you near the river's edge, a boat will pull up for you. This is your special boat and it can look any way you want it to. As your boat pulls up, you will step effortlessly into it and settle yourself very comfortably. The boat will pull away from shore and travel downstream. You will be asked to relax and enjoy the ride. You will also be asked to notice what you see as you float along the river.

After a while, your boat will pull up to shore again. You will step out onto another path that wanders through the forest to your special garden. Your garden is your own. It is unique. As you wander down the path, you will see the gardens of other people. When you get to your own garden, you will recognize it. Notice whether your garden has big walls or a fence or no border around it. Notice what fills it. What kinds and colors are the flowers? Notice other plants and animals in your garden.

You will be asked to find a comfortable place to sit in your garden. From that place you will survey your garden further. After a while, you will sense the presence of another in your garden. This is your guide. It may present itself in any form or no form. Greet your guide in the manner you feel most comfortable. (You may wish to say "hello" and nod or to give your guide a hug, or anywhere in between.) You may ask your guide to come nearer. If your guide takes a physical form, you may even ask it to come and sit beside you. This guide loves you and has only your best interests in mind.

Then you will ask your guide some very simple questions:

1. Is there a name I should use to call you?

2. What is your purpose for being with me?

3. Is there anything you want to tell me? -or- Is there anything I need to know?

4. Please allow me to feel your energy.

The last question is so that you will be able to more easily recognize the presence of your guide in the future. (There will probably be occasions when you are contacting that guide but you ask yourself whether or not that was really your guide, or your imagination, or someone else altogether. Knowing the feel of your guide's energy helps you to better distinguish what is going on.)

You will be asked to tell your guide you want to meet again soon and say good-bye. You will then leave your garden and go back to your boat for the ride home. When you feel ready, you will be asked to take a deep breath and open your eyes.

At this point, I suggest you quickly write down everything you remember from your meditation. How did your guide look? What was the name? What animals and plants did you see on your journey? What does your garden look like? What were the predominant colors of flowers and plants along your journey and in your garden? Why is your guide here for you? Was there anything unusual that you noticed during the meditation?

If you had difficulty during the meditation, make note of that as well. Did you have trouble getting to your garden? Or trouble recognizing it? Were you able to see another presence in your garden? Did you see your guide, but far in the distance? Was your guide's information clear? Did you have difficulty understanding your guide (sound garbled or unclear)? Or did you "hear" nothing in reply when you asked questions of your guide? What did your guide share with you?

I assure you, these are very common responses from people who make their first attempts to work with their guides. Many people in my classes have reported these very experiences in their meditations. I find it most common when people have fears about whether or not they will be able to contact their guides. If you had some difficulty, refer to the chapter on "trouble shooting your meditations."

Working with Your Guide

This is the second meditation, on the reverse side of your tape. Its purpose is to provide you with suggestions and relaxing background music so that you may make regular contact with your guide and receive information from it.

I suggest you follow all the same preparations for this second meditation that you did for the first, including your special affirmation. Even though you are probably more relaxed and open to making contact with your guides, you will find that most of those preparations (such as turning off the phone) will be very helpful.

In this meditation you will be asked to sit comfortably in a chair, making sure your arms and legs are not crossed. You will be asked to relax, breathe deeply, and close your eyes. Then you will to allow yourself to see and feel a light moving in a circle around your body, beginning with your feet.

You will begin to slowly draw the light up through your body. Notice the color of the light and how it feels as it passes up through your body, illuminating every part as it passes. First to your ankles. Then to your calves. Feel it passing to your knees. Now the light passes on to your thighs. Then to your groin and hips. Feel each part of your body relaxing more when the light passes to it. The light passes through your abdomen and stomach. On to your chest and back. Up to your shoulders. Feel the light passing to your upper arms, then to your elbows. Now it passes on down your forearms, to your wrists and hands.

Feel the light continuing up from your shoulders to your neck and throat. On to your chin and jaw. Then to your face, nose and ears. On to your forehead, and finally to the top of your head. Feel the light swirling around your entire body. It is beautiful and peaceful. Now feel the light coming out of the top of your head and spilling over like a fountain. You are drenched in this beautiful light.

Now you will visualize yourself on a path in the forest approaching your garden. As you near your garden, you take notice if anything external has changed (such as the fence or wall, if there is one). Then, as you enter your garden, you will be asked to notice whether or not anything within the garden has changed. These changes will be symbolic of any changes taking place within your own life.

Once you have had a look around your garden, you will be asked to seat yourself comfortably and call your guide to come near. You will wait quietly, listening to the music as the guide comes nearer. Then you will tell the guide you wish to work with it today and that you have some questions for it.

I suggest you use the following as templates for your questions until you become accustomed to asking questions of your guides.

1. Please tell me anything special I need to know right now.

2. What am I learning from this situation with my friend (or parent or boss or lover)?

3. How can I do a better job at (pick an issue you are working on)?

4. How can I live up to my highest potential
    in this(pick a subject) area?

In addition, you may wish to ask questions of a philosophical, historical nature. I
have asked one of my guides, Sung Tu, to explain what time is and how it really works, what
the akashic records really are, why are we here
in the physical plane, what happens after the
physical plane, etc. You may want to get some
of this information from your guides.

The rest of the tape will be about 12
minutes of music while you communicate with
your guide. Then you will be asked to say good
bye to your guide and prepare to leave your
garden. When you are ready, you will take a
deep breath and open your eyes. Once again, I
suggest you keep pen and paper handy so you
can quickly write down all you experienced.

Grounding

Meditation

Spirit Guides

76

Chapter Ten

Grounding Meditation

Many of you have probably heard of some variation of the grounding meditation given here. The purpose and value of this meditation is that it helps you to bring all of your various "selves" into focus in one place at one time. Some people define these various selves as your physical body, astral body, spiritual body, emotional body, etc.

I prefer to think of it as the separate parts of you that you reserve to deal with the various issues of your life. If you are worried about money, no matter how much of you is "right here, right now", you probably have a little portion of yourself "set aside" to worry about money. And if you are anxious about whether or not a certain person will call you, there is another portion set aside to worry about that. A portion of you may be worrying about the stock market or worrying about a relative's surgery. The subject of the worry doesn't matter, it is the distraction caused by the worry that matters. That is why you still feel a "nagging uneasiness" even when you are having a good time. This doesn't happen to all people, but it does happen to most.

So, if you are worried about remembering to pay the electric bill and whether or not you're going to pass an important exam, little portions of you are independently worrying about these things. The grounding meditation helps you to bring all those little fragments of yourself back together in one place and time. It is far easier to work with your guides when you have all of your parts in the same place and time.

I find the grounding meditation to be extremely useful in the morning as well. If you wake up in the morning and it seems that everything is going wrong for you (as it does to everyone occasionally), take it as a signal that you need to be grounded. Just sit down in a chair or on the edge of your bed and spend the 2 or 3 minutes necessary to do the exercise. You'll see a terrific difference in your day.

The Meditation

Sit upright in a comfortable chair or couch or on the edge of your bed. Make sure that you are not crossing your arms or legs. (You don't want to constrict your energy flow.) Close your eyes and relax. Begin by taking slow, deep breaths. Breathe smoothly in and out. Do not stop on the in breath or the out breath.

Continue breathing deeply. Focus your attention at the base of your spine. Feel a warm glow there. Allow yourself to focus your attention toward that point until you feel your energy is fully there. Begin to feel a root (like a tree) growing down through the bottom of your spine. Feel it grow through the chair and down to the floor. Then feel it growing through the floor and through any floors below that until it reaches the ground. Now feel the root growing deep into the earth. Feel it going deeper and deeper.

Begin to feel your root spreading out and growing "rootlets". Feel it expanding very wide into the earth. Continue breathing deeply. Now feel your root structure growing the fine root hairs that make it complete.

Now that your root structure is complete and spread deep and wide into the earth, allow it to remain in place while focusing your attention on the top of your head. Feel a warm glow there. Focus your attention toward that point until your attention is fully there. Begin to envision a bright light on the top of your head about the size of a silver dollar. Feel this light become an opening in the top of your head through which you can absorb energy. Imagine a shaft of beautiful white light shining down on top of you.

Allow this light to enter your body through the top of your head and circulate through your entire body. Notice how each part of you becomes illuminated with the light as it passes through. Feel how it makes you feel calm and full of energy at the same time. Allow this light to pass through you and spread through your root into the earth. Feel the light passing positive energy to you and to the earth.

Sit for a minute or two feeling this light energy pass through you into the earth. When you feel like it, turn off the light, close the opening in the top of your head and open your eyes. You are now more grounded and ready to do other meditations or proceed with your day.

You may find it useful to actually read this meditation onto a tape for yourself and play it while you make your first attempts at this meditation. Or, if you prefer, you can order our Grounding Meditation Tape. (It also has a meditation for collecting your energy on the reverse side.) If so, pause between each direction for a few seconds to give yourself the opportunity to experience what the direction asks. A little experimentation will help you find the timing that is comfortable for you.

Spirit Guides

Overcoming Fear

and Resistance

Spirit Guides

Chapter Eleven

Overcoming Fears and Resistance

Many people express strong desires to contact spirit guides and receive information from them. These very same people often have some resistance to doing just that. That resistance usually manifests itself in the form of fears or doubts. By this time, I think I've heard most of them.

Every fear we express related to working with our guides is a point of resistance for us. It becomes another reason why we "cannot" have success in this venture. In order to deal with these fears and resistances, it is important to realize that all fears are made up in our own minds. We create our own reality. We cannot create these "negative" outcomes unless we are determined to do so. I will try to deal with all of the fears I recall. Following is a listing of those fears and doubts most often expressed by students:

1. What if I don't have a guide?

This is the one I hear most often. Of course everyone does have a guide, whether you experience it as an external entity or your higher self or another aspect of yourself, you can experience a guide. Having this fear is a little like the fear some people have as children. They wonder if their parents really love them. Indeed, they wonder if anyone really loves them. They doubt it because they doubt that they are really lovable. It is the same way with a guide. The people who say they may not have a guide are those who think they may not deserve a guide. We all have guides. Some of us are more open to experiencing them. It's that simple. As you open more, you can have the joy of working with your guides.

2. I'm not psychic. What if I can't contact my guide?

This one is based on a belief in one's own limitations. Every person on this planet is capable of being psychic, whether they admit it or not. If they don't admit it, however, they are not likely to experience it. Being "psychic" is merely being able to tune in to your other senses. The most successful business executives in this country would not claim to be psychic either. However, they all have something in common. They listen to their "instinct" or their "gut feelings" when making decisions. If logic says go one way and their "gut" says to go another, they follow their "gut". I don't make any distinction at all between listening to your "gut" and being psychic. If you can listen to your "gut feelings" you can experience your psychic abilities.

3. With my luck, I'll pull in a "bad" guide.

Without sounding too sarcastic, I'd like to say this is a great example of a thought pattern which could cause a person to have less than uplifting experiences. There is no such thing as "luck". It is just a convenient excuse to keep from taking the responsibility or credit for what is going on in our lives. All of us have done this at some time in our lives. What happens is that we can create a negative cycle. Negative belief creates negative experience. Negative experience reinforces negative belief which spawns even more negative belief. By the same token, you cannot pull in a "bad" guide unless you believe you can. I know some of this sounds overly simplified, but it really is that simple. For instance, suppose you believe you can't find a mate. Your belief creates that reality -- perhaps in the form of only meeting "unavailable" people. Every time you meet another unavailable person you have a negative thought that reinforces your belief that you cannot find a mate. It may go something like this, "Ill never find a mate because everyone I meet is already attached to someone else. Just like this one." Then that thought reinforces your circumstances (your reality) and so on, ad infinitum.

4. What if I can't handle working with a guide? What if I freak out?

This is another fearful or negative thought that will only become a reality if you give it enough energy. In all my years of this work, I have never seen anyone freak out from working with their guides. I have seen a few people who freaked out because of drugs, particularly psychedelics. The use of such drugs can tear down many of the barriers we have built around us in order to have a "sane" reality. I do not recommend the use of these drugs by anyone. You can experience altered consciousness and heightened states of awareness through meditation. It may take longer, but meditation is infinitely safer and doesn't cause the physical break down that drugs can. If you are not on drugs or alcohol, and if you are not currently being treated for mental instability, I think it extremely unlikely that you would have problems coping with working with your guides.

5. How will I know it's okay to trust what my guide says?

I answer this question with the same answer I would use if you wanted to know if it is okay to trust what your next door neighbor says. I would tell you to use your own instinct. Use your own judgment. Discern the truth. You have the ability to know clearly what is your truth and what is not. Just because you receive information from a guide, it is not any more truth than information you receive from other sources. The guides are not 100% infallible. And remember, what you are receiving from them is always filtered a little by your own approach to life and your own belief system. It is highly unlikely that you will receive information from your guide that is totally outside your reality. A man whom I trained privately to work with guides is rather caustic and hard on others. The guide he works with gives him the same kind of tough lectures that he gives to others. It is obviously being filtered through his own personality. Another man I trained is gentle and nurturing to others. He experiences his guides as gentle and nurturing.

6. My guides might tell me something I don't want to hear. What do I do then?

What do you do when a friend tells you something you don't want to hear? Do you pay attention and allow yourself to see if it has a ring of truth to it? Do you become defensive? Do you deny it? Do you blame your friend for sharing the truth as he/she knows it? Do you thank your friend for telling you something you needed to hear? Your response to these questions might well be, "That depends on the circumstances and what my friend told me." You will find that response to be useful when working with guides. I don't think you will hear much that you don't want to hear. I have only met one person ever who receives "bad news" from guides. He is another man I trained privately. I'm convinced that his personality needs the bad news so he can have something to worry about and so he can have more excitement in his life by having to cope with the negative possibilities. I assume you are a basically positive person and therefore don't need to attract negative input.

7. I'm afraid I'll pull in a guide who will be critical to me like my parents (or spouse, or friends).

The fact that you are aware of your need to have a guide who is non-critical means you most likely have the situation under control. If you have attracted a lot of critical persons into your life, you may want to look at the notion that they reflect how you feel about yourself. Maybe you see yourself as imperfect because of your money, appearance, career, lifestyle, etc. If you see yourself as imperfect, you are always giving yourself little subconscious criticisms. Those people in your life are only doing you the favor of getting all that criticism out in the open so you can see your beliefs about yourself. When you change how you feel about yourself, you don't get criticized any more. In addition to looking at inner feelings about yourself, you may want to include something about your guide being positive and supportive in your special affirmation.

8. I've tried a hundred times to contact my guides and it didn't work. Why should I believe it will work now?

People tried hundreds and thousands of times to run the four-minute-mile. They failed because it was widely held to be impossible. Then one day it happened. The very next weekend three more people did it. Those three people could do it because they suddenly knew it was possible. Prior to Roger Bannister breaking the four-minute barrier for running a mile, it was thought to be impossible. If you believe something is impossible, it will be. Give yourself some positive affirmations about being able to contact your guides easily. I'm sure with that and the tape, you will find success very shortly. If the meditation doesn't work completely for you the first time, do it again when you feel like it. Keep using the first meditation a few times. You will find it gets easier with each attempt.

9. What if my guides tell me something wrong?

This is actually another version of number 5, regarding trusting what your guide says. However, I find that a significant number of people use this different wording and feel a distinction between the two. It also comes down to your definition of wrong. If your guide tells you a certain football team will win this week and they don't, then you got some information which did not come to be validated by experience. Pay attention to what you are asking from your guides, Is it something you really need to know? Are you using them just to satisfy your curiosity? Or are you using your guides to learn and grow? I find that if you are using them for casual curiosity or to predict the future, your own filters may be distorting the information according to what you want or don't want to hear.

10. How can I learn to control when I contact a guide and when I don't?

This is a question which comes from people fearful that they will suddenly be "hearing" their guides voices in the middle of a business meeting or in church or some other inappropriate place. (Kind of like Topper in the old movies. He was always being distracted by the ghosts of George and Marion Kirby at the most inopportune times.) This is another instance in which I have yet to see an actual case of guides interfering when it isn't appropriate. There is actually a universal law which people follow who don't want to incur extra karma. The rule is, simply put, "You cannot interfere in the lives of others unless they invite you to do so." If you interfere in the lives of others without invitation, you incur the karma that results from that interference. Guides are very aware of that law and have no desire to incur extra karma. Your guides won't be popping in to interfere — unless you invite them.

11. What if I don't like my guide?

What if you don't like the person you are dating? You get rid of them, right? It works the same with a guide. If you have a guide you don't like, You tell it to go away. Some people I know suggest telling a guide to "go to the light" to ensure they go to the "right place". Of course, there is another alternative. You can tell your guide that you don't want it around unless it is going to present a different personality to you. You may be able to successfully work it out. Keep in mind, however, if you are attracting into your life lots of people or guides you don't like, you may want to look at your inner beliefs.

12. What if my guide doesn't like me?

I have never seen a case where someone attracted a guide that didn't like them. If you do, I would guess it is a reflection of your own attitudes toward yourself. You may be filtering your guides message to tell you what you are trying to tell yourself. I cannot even imagine a guide that didn't like the person it was working with. After all, your guide is here to help you.

Why would you want to take a lot of interest in and help a person you don't even like? Doesn't make sense, does it?

13. How can I tell the difference between my guide, my higher self, and my own thoughts?

This is one that takes a little practice. However, I find that my own thoughts are in the same sort of language structure as I use to speak and write. My language style is fairly casual. My guides, however "speak" to me in a much more formal style. Most people I know make some distinction in the "speech" style of themselves and their guides. As for the difference between me and my higher self, I don't make a distinction. It is all me as far as I'm concerned. Another way to distinguish is the feeling you get when you receive messages or thoughts. There is a certain energy I can feel when a particular guide is with me. That is why we ask you to experience your guide's energy in the first meditation. It is another way for you to tell the difference.

14. People might think I'm crazy.

The fear of what other people think is very powerful, indeed. That's why our moms always told us to wear clean underwear in case we got hit by a bus. Mom was worried that in the emergency room, someone might be more concerned with the cleanliness of your underwear than with saving your life. (I have always thought that if you got hit by a bus, your underwear probably wouldn't be clean anymore anyway.) There isn't anything I can do or say to make you less concerned about what other people think of you. Perhaps you won't share certain aspects of your life with others until you feel safe in doing so. If you are worried about what others will think and you also want to pursue this program of working with your guides, you may want to keep it to yourself. However, you are not crazy for wanting to contact guides. There are lots of others out there. Some of them are in the closet because of the same fear. Others are more open about it.

15. I might think I'm crazy.

It is possible that you will at least doubt what is going on when you begin to experience work with your guides. Everyone I have ever known (including me) has doubted that it was "real". We constantly asked the question, "Is this real or my imagination?" at first. You might do this too. If so, it is perfectly normal. It can take a while to adjust to a new experience of reality. Even those of us who had long before accepted the idea that working with guides was good and normal and even fun, found that we doubted it all when we began to actually experience it. I personally kept thinking it was too good to be true. I was having so much fun. I liked it so much, that I thought I must be making it all up in my mind. It helped a lot to meet other people having almost identical experiences to mine. I suggest you try to find other people for support if you doubt your sanity.

Trouble Shooting

Problems

Chapter Twelve

Trouble Shooting Problems

It is possible that your first attempt at meeting and working with a guide will be a little disappointing to you. No matter what your problem, it is something that can be overcome fairly easily. Following are the problems I have most often encountered with students and some ways to deal with them.

Having Trouble Seeing Your Guide

This is one of the very most common complaints in the beginning stages of working with your guide. It is hard for someone just starting out to believe that he/she really has a guide when the guide can't be seen. Remember that your guide may not feel the need to present itself to you in physical form. If that seems to be so and you need a physical image, ask your guide to let you ""see" it.

If you feel the difficulty is within you, then try this exercise. Get in a comfortable position. Breathe deeply. Close your eyes. See yourself back in your beautiful garden. Relax, find yourself at peace and comfortable there. As you are sitting there, ask your guide to enter the garden. Remain relaxed and peaceful. Feel positive energy coming from your guide. Then notice there is a photo lying next to you, face down. Slowly reach out and pick up the photo. Turn it over to see the photo. What you see in the photo is a picture of your guide. You may want to try this more than once if the first picture is blurred or fuzzy. Give yourself a little time (a few hours or a few days) between at-tempts. Don't pressure yourself to "see" your guide. The less pressure, the more easy it is for you to "see".

Having Trouble Hearing Your Guide

Many people report not "hearing" at all or hearing a "garbled" sound. Some say it is like hearing someone talking at a distance or through a wall. You can tell they are talking but you can't make out what they are saying. I think the easiest way to deal with this is to relax. When you next meet with your guide, ask it to speak more clearly. Ask it to help you understand what it is trying to say to you.

If it is still hard to hear, try this exercise. Visualize yourself sitting in a quiet corner of your garden. Relax and breathe deeply. Notice you have one of those small portable radios. You will use this radio to listen to your guide. When your guide begins to speak, allow yourself to hear the guide speak through the radio speaker or through the head phones (whichever you find most comfortable). If the voice is faint or distant, slowly turn up the volume on the radio.

As you slowly turn up the volume, notice your guide's voice being louder and clearer. If your guide sounds "garbled", slowly work the tuner part of the radio. Begin turning the tuning dial slowly until your guide's voice becomes clear as a bell. You may have to tune in an out, past the sound of your guide in both directions to finely tune in the voice. (Just like tuning in a station on the radio.) Don't be frustrated. Relax and take your time, slowly turning the tuning knob one way and then the other, if necessary. You should begin to hear your guide much more clearly.

Having Trouble Following the Meditation

This can mean any one of several things. For instance, I have seen people who had trouble following a meditation because they were distracted by thoughts about things going on in their lives. They weren't relaxed enough to let go of all the daily distractions. If this is true for you, try a little deep breathing, counting your breaths. Count up to eight, then start over. If you focus your mind on counting your breaths, you can't be thinking of anything else. This will help you practice "letting go" of all the difficulties of the day. Doing the grounding meditation will also help you let go of your distractions. Once you become more adept at letting go, try the meditation again.

I have often seen people who thought they weren't doing the meditation right because they ended up somewhere else, instead of where the guided meditation suggested. If this happens to you, I suggest you go with it, rather than trying to conform to the suggestions. You are going where you need to go. I once had a man in class who did the countdown and went to the meadow. But when I suggested he enter the forest, he found himself rising up and flying over everything. Instead of the forest, he went to a big wheat field on top of a hill. He stayed in the wheat field instead of going to his garden, too. This fellow thought he had "screwed up" because he didn't make it to his garden. I didn't think he "screwed up" at all.

He went where he needed to go and instead of meeting one guide, as I suggest in the meditation, he met three guides in the field! If this kind of deviation happens to you, don't get too caught up in trying to do exactly what the tape says. Follow your own urges if they are that strong. Remember, you can always use your tape over and over, so you can see whether you go to the garden or to various other places each time.

Spirit Guides

New Guides

Chapter Thirteen

New Guides

From time to time people experience new, additional guides entering their lives, or what we call a guidance change. Whether your new guide is an "add-on" or a replacement, it may require a little sensitivity on your part to know what is going on. You may just feel that things are different when you meditate. I have gone for a spiritual reading and had the reader tell me I was experiencing a change in guidance. I realized that I was feeling some shifting going on with my guides, but I hadn't really pinned it down as meaning a change in guidance. When someone else pointed it out, I could see more clearly that was the case.

Any time you begin to feel things are

different with you and your guides, even if you can't really pin down what the difference is, you may want to check to see if you are getting new guides. To do this, you may wish to return to side one of the tape, Meeting Your Guide and go through the meditation again (even if you have been using side two for quite a while) to meet any new guide(s) that may be around. If you are using it for this purpose, I suggest you alter your special affirmation to say you are open to meeting your new guides.

If you go through this exercise, you will have a sense of whether there is new guidance for you. You are more likely to "see" and "hear" your new guide right away if you have been working regularly with previous guides. In any case, you will get a feeling about whether or not there is a new guide waiting for you in your garden.

If you don't want to go all the way through the exercise of going to your garden and all of the steps in between, you can try the following exercise. If you are already comfortable with relaxing in meditation without going through the colored numbers, then do so. Relax and breathe deeply. Visualize yourself walking through an enchanted forest. Everything there is magical and beautiful. You feel safe and happy as you walk through the forest. The path you are on often curves in one direction or another. Sometimes, when you are nearing a curve, you cannot see what is around the corner until you are actually in the middle of the curve.

As you are walking along the winding path, begin to think about your new guide. You wonder who it is, how it will present itself, etc. Then, just as you are rounding a curve, you meet another on the path coming toward you. This is your guide. It has arrived to greet you. Your thinking about it has drawn it to you. Talk to your guide as you do to your other guides, asking questions and listening to the answers.

If you have gotten to the point that you are writing what your guides are saying to you in meditation, do the same with this new guide. Write down what your guide is saying. You may want to ask some specific questions of your guide which are quite similar to those we suggest in the taped meditation. Ask your guide why it is here for you and why it came now (rather than another time). Ask your guide if it is replacing another guide or if it is an additional guide. If it is a "replacement", ask if there will be a transition period in which both the old and new guides will work with you. If it is a replacement, you may want to ask for the significance of the timing. And of course, you may want to ask if there is a special message for you or anything you need to know.

If you go through these various processes and find no new guide there for you, then maybe it is not time just yet. Perhaps you are sensing a change which is coming in the near future. We often feel the energy of something moving toward us long quite some time before the event actually occurs.

Channeling

Spirit Guides

Chapter Fourteen

Channeling

There are books appearing on the market on the subject of channeling with great regularity these days. Some of them are very good. For in depth information on the subject, I suggest you look over those books. However, a book about communicating with spirit guides would not be complete without some information on channeling. I believe that when you go from your initial work with guides to written and oral communication that you are indeed doing your own channeling.

What is Channeling?

Channeling is a word used far and wide to

mean many different things. The definitions of channeling depend entirely on the belief system of the person defining the word. To make it even more complicated, there are subsets of the term. There is "trance" channeling, "conscious" channeling, "sleep" channeling, "spontaneous" channeling, "spiritual" channeling, etc. What I tell you here will be my definitions based on my beliefs. They may or may not differ from what you have read or heard elsewhere.

The above question is by far and away the most asked question I hear in classes and in group channeling sessions. There is so much confusion surrounding it that many people aren't clear at all about it. (This is not helped at all by the propaganda put out by people who want to thwart new age spiritual growth.) And of course, there are many people who have very specific ideas about what is and what is not channeling.

I define channeling as:

"The activity of bringing forth information which was previously beyond one's conscious awareness." This means that you have the effect of accessing information without being aware of the information content before hand. I believe a great example of channeling was

Wolfgang Amadeus Mozart. He would write music as it came to his thoughts. He didn't have to "make it up" from experience. He wrote without corrections. He just spontaneously wrote what he was "hearing" in his head.

Some people use a drinking straw as a metaphor for a channel. They say the channel (the person channeling) brings forth information and it is passed through that person much like a beverage is passed through a straw when you sip on it. I believe this is generally true. Many people who channel (myself included) do not remember what information passed through during the channeling session. For this reason, we tape our sessions or have someone act as scribe, carefully writing it all down. We then listen to the tape or read the transcription in order to receive the information and remember it ourselves.

I believe the reason we don't remember it at the time is that we are accessing information from a "region" we are not in contact with consciously. Whether that "region" is some aspect of ourselves, such as the higher self, or whether it is something outside ourselves, such as guides and spirit entities is subject to much debate. I am not really convinced there is a difference. I think we choose to experience things differently because of our various basic beliefs, but I'm not sure there is truly a difference.

For instance, I believe we create our own reality. All of it. All of the time. However, I still frequently experience it as something happening to me, coming from outside of me. Even though it appears to be generated outside of me, I believe it really is generated within me, a part of me somehow. There is no difference between what is created by me and what appears to be coming at me from outside of me. It is just a matter of how I experience it.

Why is the Information Different from Different Channels?

Some people become confused when they discover that information from various channels is different. They want to know who is correct. It is important to first examine what you mean by different before we can discuss that question. Differences in information channeled happen at many levels. First, most of the information you hear from any of the famous channels is really the same, perhaps in a different format.

The Seth information channeled by Jane

Roberts, the Lazaris information channeled by Jach Pursel, the Ramtha information channeled by J.Z. Knight, the Orin information channeled by Sanaya Roman have very similar messages. They all talk about how you create your own reality, that you have all the power of the universe at your disposal, that happiness can be yours at any moment, that the physical world is a learning ground, that you can have anything you truly want if you let go of your limitations. Perhaps they present the information in different terms or different formats, but to my mind the message is essentially the same. If you are confused by differences in ways of presentation, then allow yourself the opportunity to be with the information they present and begin to notice how much it is all the same message.

I believe that the real messages given by various masters such as Lao Tsu, Jesus of Nazareth, Gautama Buddha, Zoroaster, etc., were essentially the same. I also believe that the messages were delivered in very different contexts and styles because of the various cultures in which they were operating. Different cultures are going to understand concepts presented in very different manners. Many people today believe the messages of all these masters were different. They also believe that some or one of them is correct and the rest of them are wrong. These people are looking at the information on a different level than I am. That is their choice and I honor it. I also want to point out that your own orientation toward something will determine how you experience it.

There is another level at which some people are confused by the messages of famous channels. This is the level at which the information being received is being filtered by their own beliefs and attitudes. (The vast majority of the channels will pass through information that is only compatible with their own belief systems.) A good example is in the area of their predictions for the earth. Some of them say we are in for very big upheavals and physical disasters. Others say the upheavals will not be physical, but economic and political. Still others say there is nothing to be concerned about, that the earth and its systems are always in states of flux and change, that there will always be a certain amount of "natural disasters" because of the nature of the earth, and that the economic and political systems are also in constant change.

I would say they are all accessing the same information or something very similar. It is just their own orientation toward the information that makes it sound different. And their orientation toward the information will depend upon their own basic core beliefs. For instance, let us assume that three different channels are passing through information about the earth. They are all accessing information relating to the fact that the earth is dynamic, not static. It is in constant change, not stagnation. Sometimes the change appears to be very big and other times not so big.

Suppose one of the channels has a strong inner belief in the concept of Armageddon and the time of massive upheaval. He will access information about "earth changes" and color it with his or her own filter so that the translation of the information says there is great disaster and upheaval to come. Another one might have a strong inner belief that we are headed toward economic disaster or war. Her filter will color the information accordingly. She will interpret the information as being economic, political and social upheavals. And a third one may carry an inner belief that there is never any danger because everything happens according to some divine plan and that everything is always moving and shifting as part of growth. He will filter and color the information to be a message that there is nothing to fear, everyone is in the right place at the right time, etc.

I'm not saying this "filtering" usually takes place on a conscious level. In fact, it hardly ever does. But the person will still act as a filter for the information received. That person's brain function, vocabulary, etc., will have a great deal of bearing on what he or she is able to channel. I channel a guide named Sung Tu. This guide presents himself to me as he was in a Chinese incarnation. However, if I were channeling for someone who wanted to have Sung Tu speak to him in Chinese, it would not happen. The reason: I don't have a knowledge of Chinese myself. Since I am present and I don't leave my body during the channeling, I act as a filter or limiter on the information. I believe this is true with nearly every channel you meet.

Where is the Personality of the Channeler?

For quite some time the prevailing information on the whereabouts of channelers' own personalities or souls when they were channeling was as follows. They were "gone" to some other dimension or to some other reality during the channeling. They would describe it as leaving their bodies, often passing the spirit of the entity to be channeled as they were leaving. Some would say they went to a very bright light. Others would say they were in some sort of suspended animation. Almost all of them would report that they could not remember at all what was said during the channeling session.

I remember when I was told many years ago that I would be doing vocal channeling for people. I flatly denied the possibility. I wasn't at all interested in leaving my body and loaning it out to another spirit. Because I believed that was the only way for people to channel, I rejected it altogether. However, when I actually began to experience channeling, I discovered that I didn't go anywhere at all. I stayed right here in my body. I experienced contact with my guide telepathically. It was as if my guide fed me "pure" information (not in words) and it somehow got translated inside my brain and came out as words.

I actually hear what is being said by Sung Tu (using my voice) when I am channeling his energy. However, I don't remember it at all when I am through. I believe this is because in opening up my intuitive center to work with my guides, I also "close" the part that analyzes, categorizes and files information away into memory for future access. If I kept my analytical self wide open, I would be filtering the information with my conscious thoughts. (I said earlier that I think we all filter it with unconscious thoughts. Think how limited the information would be if we added the conscious mind to filter the thoughts as well.)

Can Everyone Channel?

I believe most certainly that everyone is capable of channeling information at some level. There isn't some special "gift" given to those who channel that other people don't have. Channelers have been willing to extend their experiences, to work with their guides, to practice channeling. Like any other discipline, it gets better with practice. With practice, the channeler begins to relax, to trust more what is going on, to have less resistance and to act less as a conscious filter.

We all have the innate capability to channel, but we may still not be able to experience it. When I was told that I would be doing channeling some day, I didn't believe it. I had a great deal of resistance to it. As long as I kept very high resistance, I couldn't channel. You can't do something if you are resisting it a great deal. But, over time I became comfortable with the idea and my resistance began to drop. When my resistance had sufficiently abated, I began to experience channeling. Many of you who wish to channel, but feel you haven't yet achieved the state of being or ability required may actually be resisting it more than you think.

Of course, another barrier to experiencing channeling is one's own beliefs and fears. There are people who were told all their lives that if they hear "voices" or communicate with non-physical beings they are either crazy or talking to the devil. Either of those beliefs can create a lot of internal barriers even if you think you have out-grown them.

However, if you are willing to look within and clear any barriers you may have, you can channel just as easily and just as well as anyone else. It will require some patience and discipline, and most of all, trust in yourself. If you can muster those up, you've got it made — no matter what your goals are in life. Perhaps you can visualize your barriers as hurdles and see yourself jumping them. Or maybe you wish to visualize your barriers as locked doors and see yourself opening them with the magic key.

Many People Channeling One Guide

There is a lot of controversy surrounding this issue. I've seen several cases in which many people are channeling the same guidance or wisdom. The Michael channelings are perhaps one of the most famous examples. Several different people seem to cooperate in channeling the Michael energy in order to bring through its wisdom.

It is also very common with people who are channeling a traditional religious figure. I've met many people who say they are channeling the wisdom of Jesus Christ, the Virgin Mary, Quan Yin, John the Baptist, the Archangel Gabriel, etc. And they all feel comfortable with the idea that any number of other people may be accessing that wisdom on their own. I've also met several people who say they channel wisdom from some other famous people such as Albert Einstein, Nicola Tesla, Buckminster Fuller, etc. They, too feel that anyone can access these sources of wisdom.

If you believe (as I do) that we are much more than just physical human beings and that we have unlimited potential and power, then you might also believe that any of us can access any wisdom at any time. If you also understand that guidance in spiritual realms is not limited to the physical barriers of being in one place at one time, then you might also believe that it is possible for two people in two separate locations to be channeling the same entity at the same time.

A few channels claim they are the sole channel for a particular entity. They say anyone else who claims to be channeling that entity is incorrect and that the true wisdom of that entity can only come through the one channel. I believe this is an excellent example of the channel acting as a filter for the guide. I personally believe all wisdom is available to all people at all times. I don't believe you must consult with that particular channel in order to access that particular wisdom. (It might be much easier to do it that way, however. If someone else already has considerable experience and practice working with a particular guide's energy and its wisdom, you might find it easier to consult through that channel rather than work on it yourself.)

It is easy to understand how a person's own filter might get involved and have the channeled entity declare this particular channel as its sole communication with the earth plane. It certainly reduces certain potential hassles. If several people are claiming to channel a particular guide, and you have the variations which will naturally come through because of the filters of the various channels, argument could break out over which channel is correct. If, however, you have already established a monopoly on that particular wisdom and people have accepted this, there will be no argument. Anyone else claiming to channel your guide will be dismissed as a phony. In addition, there is a certain obvious financial advantage to having sole proprietorship of a guide.

I'm not trying to say that I think people who claim to be sole channelers of a guide are less than professional and forthcoming. I'm just saying it is natural for their filters (at a subconscious level) to color what is said in order to protect them from any perceived threats or insecurities. People who don't necessarily have those particular fears or insecurities don't generally claim to be the only person through whom an entity can speak.

Written Channeling

Some people call this automatic writing. I call this written channeling rather than automatic writing for a couple of reasons. First, the term automatic writing implies certain things which may or may not occur during written channeling. Most of the descriptions I have read and people I have witnessed doing automatic writing have the characteristic of being "beyond their control." Many people who do automatic writing claim it is as if some other being is controlling their hand. The automatic writer is just watching in amazement as his or her hand is flying across the page or is in a deep trance and remembers nothing. This is not necessarily true with someone who is doing written channeling, though it is possible.

The second reason I call it written channeling is that it takes some of the "mystique" out of it. By its nature, automatic writing appears to be restricted to a chosen few, and those few generally feel they had no part in the choosing. Written channeling is available to all and you can choose to do it. It seems to be the least intimidating of all the forms of channeling available. (Unless, of course, you are intimidated by writing, which a few people are.) It is private, so no one else needs to witness what you are doing.   It is less distracting than hearing your own voice, or what seems like a different voice coming out of your mouth.

If you want to try your hand at written channeling, I suggest the following procedure. First, listen to the first side of the tape (Meeting Your Guide) enough times to feel you have made solid contact with a guide. Continue working with your guide a few times using side two of the tape (Working with Your Guide) until you feel you have clear communication from your guide.

Write down everything you can recall after each experience. This is the first stage of beginning written channeling.

Once you have a clear line of communication with your guide, prepare for your written channeling by placing a pen and a tablet or a few sheets of paper on a table in front of you. (Use a table that is a good height for writing.) Seat yourself at the table and breathe deeply to relax. Begin your own process of connecting with your guide. Once you have made contact, ask your guide what you need to know right now. You could also ask your guide to answer a specific question that does not have "yes" or "no" as an obvious answer.

Sit quietly after asking the question. When you start hearing an answer from your guide, start writing down what you hear, word for word. It is just like taking dictation. If you feel you cannot write fast enough, ask your guide to slow down. Continue writing down what you "hear" from your guide. At first, you will hear a few words or a sentence or two and then you will write them down. After a while, you will find yourself able to write what the guide says almost immediately after it is said. Then you will find that you are writing it as you hear it. There will no longer be a gap in time between hearing it and writing it down. If you allow yourself to do written channeling for 10 or 15 minutes a day, every day, you will find yourself making great strides in only a week.

Spoken Channeling

Relatively few people ever learn to do spoken channeling. There is certainly a greater number of speaking channels around than there used to be, and more seem to be turning up daily. However, the number will probably always remain small relative to the numbers of people who are learning to work with their guides. It is seen as more "risky". And of course anything that is more public in nature carries more perceived "risk." The perceived risk is usually in the form of the judgment of others and the fear of what they will think. Another reason of course, is the old standard fear all of us carry within — the fear of being wrong. Worrying about being wrong is bad enough, but compounding that fear with worrying that other people will know it when we are "wrong" causes many of us not to take action.

I'm not saying all this to frighten you. In fact, I'm saying it to let you know that everyone is working with the same fears you are. Some of us let those fears paralyze us and others don't. Assuming you want to go forward and experience spoken channeling, following are some ideas which may help you.

First, I suggest you spend a few weeks (at least) doing the written channeling. This will enable you to become accustomed to working with your guide closely and to receiving messages. Once you feel comfortable with this, you are ready to begin the process of learning vocal channeling. I feel it is very important for you to do this with a friend at first. Not because there is any danger, but a friend can be of great help in coaxing you along and giving you certain suggestions. A friend can operate a tape recorder or act as scribe when you are doing the spoken channeling. A friend can also ask questions of the entity you are channeling so that your guide has someone to respond to. And a friend will help you keep from falling sound asleep if you choose to begin spoken channeling by lying down. Ask a friend who is also interested in working with guides. Make sure it is a friend you trust and feel comfortable with.

Sit in a chair or lie in a comfortable place. (Make sure you have made all the preparations listed in the chapter called Preparation to Work with Your Guides, especially the ones which help you avoid interruptions.) Relax and breathe deeply. Have your friend observe your relaxation. The friend should also ask you to tell him/ her when you are in contact with a guide. Once you have indicated contact, your friend should ask you to describe what you are "seeing" or experiencing. Without trying to be too technical, tell your friend what you are experiencing.

Most likely, part of your experience will include "hearing" someone talking or knowing someone is getting ready to talk. Your friend should ask you to repeat what you hear. At first you will hear a sentence or two and then repeat it. After a while you will find the time between hearing it and repeating it becomes lesser and lesser until you are hearing and speaking simultaneously.

When you are first experiencing spoken channeling, you may become tense and frustrated. This is usually because you are worried about getting it right. That is why a friend you can trust is very important. You can relax more with this person. Ask your friend to monitor your status while you are first attempting your spoken channeling. If your friend senses that you are tensing up (and therefore resisting the process), he/she should suggest that you take a deep breath and relax. Your friend should also suggest that you can take it slowly if you want, that there is no rush.

Allow yourself plenty of time to become accustomed to the process before you expect significant information. Your first attempt may last only a few minutes. That is fine. That is normal. As you practice, you will become more comfortable with the process and more trusting of what is going on. If you can practice a couple of times a week at first, you will find yourself progressing noticeably.

Remember

to Ask

Chapter Fifteen

Remember to Ask

This may seem obvious, but I find that everyone I know, myself included, has to be reminded to ask our guides for help. (Or for information or guidance or wisdom or whatever.)   No matter how long we have been doing this work, we still forget to ask for help whenever a situation arises that we are having trouble with.   Sometimes I find myself up against a brick wall, unable to figure out why I am meeting so much resistance with a situation.   Then a friend will say, "Why don't you ask your guides?"   I always respond with "Oh, yeah," rather sheepishly.   Here I am, a person whose livelihood is derived from working with guides and yet I forget to ask.

As I mentioned in the chapter entitled *Overcoming Fears and Resistance* (Page 83), part of the universal law is that you take on karma of a person or situation if you interfere. My experience has been that spirit guides are keenly aware of this. They will wait until you ask before diving in to help or change the situation. They have enough karma of their own and they know it. They don't have any desire to create any more karma.

Therefore, you shouldn't expect your guide to follow you around like a babysitter or saviour and help you all the time unbidden. However, my experience is that spirit guides are anxious to help you and will jump to it any time you remember to ask. I've never seen one ignore a call for help.

When in doubt, ask. If you are not sure whether or not one of your guides can help you with a certain situation or issue, ask. That is the easiest way to find out. If you ask and feel you are not getting any help, ask why. It may be that your own higher self is working this out with you in its own way and that any "outside" help would cause difficulty.

It also may be that your guides are not here for that particular purpose. And of course, it can also be a reflection of an inner resistance to accept help. Whatever it is, I am sure you will get a satisfactory answer (that is, if you are able to receive answers from your guides at that point).

About Protection

Chapter Sixteen

About Protection

I have taught many classes on working with spirit guides and on psychic development. Occasionally, the issue of protection arises. One time, when a friend attended a class and was later giving me critique on it, he took me to task for not spending a lengthy amount of time on protection. (In fact, I usually omitted the subject altogether unless someone mentioned it in class.)

I feel a need to cover the subject briefly herein because some of you may be concerned about the subject or you may have heard some-thing from someone else about it. I personally believe that you create your own reality, every single aspect of it. That includes any need for protection. If you don't think you need protection, you don't.

I had a business partner several years ago who lived in very high security condominiums. I lived in a stand alone house on the street. To get into his apartment, you had to go through security doors, ring a buzzer, pass video cameras, etc. When you finally got to his door, there were three locks on it. My place had one lock, which I often forgot to set. My business partner lived in this high security environment because he wanted to ensure that he and his belongings would be safe. (I always assumed that I and my belongings were safe.) Within an 18 month period, he was burglarized three times in three different apartments. Each time he had moved to an even more "secure" apartment. In good weather, I sometimes forgot to close my door, let alone lock it. I was never robbed.

I am not trying to state that I am superior in any way to my former partner. No, indeed. I am just using that situation to illustrate my point. You don't need protection unless you think you do. Because my partner was so concerned with security, he created exactly what he was trying so hard to prevent. Because

I didn't believe anyone would ever rob me, I didn't create it.

This same principle works with protection when working with guides. If you think you need protection, then give yourself some. I hesitate to think how much more difficulty my partner would have had if he carried the fear of being robbed but did nothing to protect himself.

There are those people who say you must be very careful when opening yourself up to the spiritual world because you will be vulnerable to "evil" spirits as well as "good" ones. If you believe this, protect yourself!

I personally don't believe in "evil" spirits. Because I don't believe in them, I've never encountered one. My reality will always reflect my inner beliefs. So does yours. If you have a little fear or doubt about this, then my advice is to do the prudent thing and protect yourself. What feels like a little fear has just as much pulling power as a big fear.

The three most common methods people use for protection are prayer, smudging and white light.

Prayer

This method is somewhat obvious. It involved saying a prayer to invoke protection. The Unity Church has a prayer for protection. The people with the Church of Tzaddi pass out little cards with the Prayer for Protection on them. That prayer goes like this:

The light of God surrounds me.

The love of God enfolds me.

The power of God protects me.

The presence of God watches over me.

Wherever I am, God is.

So be it.

Amen.

If you wish to use the prayer, say it before doing any spiritual work. Some people also say it in the morning when arising and in the evening when retiring.

Smudging

Smudging is a technique passed down by

Native Americans and some other Shamanistic traditions. The idea is to "smudge" the room where you will be working with a special smoke (most people burn sage). The smoke is supposed to clear out the room of any negative energies or evil spirits.

You can buy bundles of sage that have been tied together. You light one end of the bundle, wait a minute, then blow it out as with incense. The sage will then produce smoke. You can walk about the room, spreading the smoke to all areas. When you are through, extinguish the sage completely. If you wish to combine this ritual with the prayer for protection, you may do so.

White Light

The idea of using white light to protect yourself comes from the old axiom, "Where there is light, there can be no darkness." Most people view the positive or good energies as being from the light and negative or evil energies as being from darkness.

To use the white light, close your eyes and take a deep breath. Visualize yourself being surrounded by a beautiful, brilliant shaft of white light. As the white light surrounds you, know that this light is your protector and nothing unwanted can penetrate this light. Sit with the light surrounding you until you feel comfortable with it. Do not turn the light off when you open your eyes. Just know that it is there with you. Some people choose to combine the white light with the prayer.

Whether you use one of these or any combination of them, you will probably find them to be useful if you want to feel protected while you work with spirit.

About the Author

Victoria Young has been involved in Spiritual or Metaphysical pursuits since September of 1961, when she had an out-of-body experience while clinically "dead" in a hospital emergency room. Ms. Young believes it was one of her guides who "pushed" her back into her body at that time. Because she was a week shy of her 12th birthday when this happened, Victoria did not have a philosophical or intellectual understanding of the experience. Instead, she found herself following urges. Within a week of leaving the hospital, she bought her first deck of tarot cards and an astrology book. These actions were the beginning of a life-long pursuit of spiritual understanding.

For many years her spiritual growth, learning and sharing were part of her "private life" as she went on to pursue a career in business. Victoria obtained a Master's Degree in International Management and worked as a manager in Fortune 500 corporations. All the

---

while she was giving readings and continuing her study and practice during her "spare" time.

During the last five years of her "corporate life," Victoria began to be more "public" about her activities and offered several regular classes. In the Spring of 1986, Victoria began her full-time dedication to spiritual work.

Ms. Young has channeled a great deal of information for herself and her clients. She hopes to eventually publish some of this channeled information.

Victoria's work is based on her belief that we all create our own reality according to what we need to learn and experience. "Our own higher wisdom is constantly setting us up in situations that allow us to confront our beliefs about reality. Where our beliefs are negative and limited, we experience pain and limitation. Where our beliefs are positive and expansive, we experience joy and power."

Ms. Young lives with her son, Justin Alexander, in Colorado.

NOTES

NOTES

NOTES

NOTES

NOTES

NOTES

NOTES

NOTES